How To Celebrate Birthday Party

Joseph Williams

Published by Joseph Williams, 2024.

HOW TO CELEBRATE BIRTHDAY PARTY

First edition. March 7, 2024.

Written by Joseph Williams.

Table of Contents

Chapter 1 1

Chapter 2 9

Chapter 3 17

Chapter 4 23

Chapter 5 29

Chapter 6 37

Chapter 7 43

Chapter 8 49

Chapter 9 55

Conclusion 61

How To Celebrate Birthday Party

The Simple Guide to Learning Proper Ways To Celebrate Birthday Party

Joseph Williams

Disclaimer

While every precaution has been taken in the preparation of this book, the publisher assumes no responsibility for errors or omissions, or for damages resulting from the use of the information contained herein.

How To Celebrate Birthday Party: The Simple Guide How To Celebrate Birthday Party

First edition.

Table of Contents

D isclaimer

Copyright © Joseph Williams 2024. All Rights Reserved

Table of Contents
Foreword
Introduction

The Power of Celebration
The Significance of Birthday Parties

Chapter 1

Planning the Perfect Party

Choosing the Right Venue

Decorations that Wow

Navigating Guest Lists and RSVPs

The Art of Timing: When to Start and End the Celebration

If you have specific areas you'd like to explore further or particular details to emphasize, please let me know.

Chapter 2

Themes and Creative Concepts

Unleashing Your Imagination

Thematic Elements that Resonate

Timeless Classics

Trendy and Unique Themes

If you have specific areas you'd like to explore further or particular details to emphasize, please let me know.

Chapter 3

Culinary Delights

A Feast for the Senses

Tailoring Menus to Suit Every Palate

If you have specific areas you'd like to explore further or particular details to emphasize, please let me know.

Cake Matters: The Centerpiece of Celebration

If you have specific areas you'd like to explore further or particular details to emphasize, please let me know.

Chapter 4

Entertainment Extravaganza
Music and Mood
Games and Activities for All Ages
Hiring Entertainment Professionals

Chapter 5

Capturing the Moments

Photography Essentials

DIY Photo Booths and Backdrops

If there are specific aspects you'd like to delve into further or particular details to emphasize, please let me know.

Creating Lasting Memories

Chapter 6

Inclusive Celebrations
Celebrating Diverse Backgrounds and Cultures
All-Ages-Friendly Activities

Chapter 7

Gifts and Gratitude
Thoughtful Gift Ideas
Navigating Thank-You Notes

Chapter 8

Navigating Challenges
Managing Unexpected Hiccups
Handling Differing Expectations

Chapter 9

Sustainable Celebrations
Environmentally Friendly Practices
Reducing Waste without Compromising Fun

Conclusion

Note: This concluding chapter provides a summary and reflection on the key aspects discussed throughout the book, fostering a sense of closure while encouraging continued commitment to sustainable practices.

Foreword

IN A WORLD BUSTLING with routines and responsibilities, we often find solace in the joyous moments that punctuate our lives. Birthdays, in particular, stand as beacons of celebration, reminding us to embrace the simple yet profound act of marking the passage of time. In "How to Celebrate a Birthday Party," the esteemed author takes us on a delightful journey, unraveling the art of turning ordinary moments into extraordinary memories.

With a keen understanding of the human spirit, the author not only shares practical tips on planning and executing unforgettable birthday celebrations but also delves into the deeper significance of these cherished occasions. This book goes beyond the logistics of party planning; it becomes a guide to infusing each celebration with genuine warmth, connection, and the unmistakable magic that lingers in the air when people come together to honor a life.

As we navigate the pages of this book, we discover that the author is not just a purveyor of party wisdom but a storyteller weaving tales of laughter, camaraderie, and the timeless joy that accompanies a well-celebrated birthday. Through anecdotes, thoughtful insights, and expert advice, the reader is invited to embark on a transformative journey—one where each birthday becomes an opportunity to create enduring memories and strengthen the bonds that make life truly extraordinary.

So, whether you are a seasoned party planner or a newcomer to the world of birthday festivities, "How to Celebrate a Birthday Party" is your trusted companion. With its blend of practical advice and heartfelt wisdom, this book stands as a testament to the enduring power of celebration in fostering a life rich in connection, joy, and the enduring spirit of celebration.

Get ready to embark on a journey that transcends the ordinary, as this book unlocks the secrets to not just celebrating birthdays but embracing life's beautiful tapestry one heartfelt celebration at a time.

Cheers to a life well celebrated!

Introduction

The Power of Celebration

THE POWER OF CELEBRATION: Unveiling the Magic Within

In the tapestry of human existence, few threads are as vibrant and universally woven as the celebration of life's moments. "The Power of Celebration" seeks to unravel the layers of joy, connection, and profound significance that encompass our collective celebrations. As we embark on this journey, we will delve into the essence of celebration, exploring its impact on individuals, communities, and the human spirit.

Chapter 1: The Essence of Celebration
- Defining Celebration: More Than Mere Festivities
- The Psychological Impact: How Celebrations Shape Our Well-being

Chapter 2: The Cultural Tapestry of Celebrations
- Diverse Traditions: A Global Panorama of Celebratory Practices
- Rituals and Symbolism: Understanding the Cultural Roots of Celebration

Chapter 3: Celebrating Milestones
- Birthdays, Weddings, and Beyond: The Rhythms of Life
- Navigating Transitions: How Celebrations Mark Change and Growth

Chapter 4: Social Connection and Community Building
- The Social Glue: How Celebrations Strengthen Bonds
- Community Celebrations: Fostering Unity and Belonging

Chapter 5: The Science of Celebration
- Neurological Impact: How Celebrations Affect the Brain
- The Role of Dopamine: Unraveling the Biochemistry of Joy

Chapter 6: Creating Unforgettable Memories
- The Art of Mindful Celebration
- Capturing Moments: Photography and the Preservation of Memories

This is just a glimpse of the expansive landscape we will explore in "The Power of Celebration." As we navigate through the chapters, we will uncover the secrets, traditions, and science that make celebration a potent force in shaping our lives.

IF YOU HAVE SPECIFIC areas you'd like to dive deeper into or particular topics you want to focus on, please let me know.

The Significance of Birthday Parties

THE SIGNIFICANCE OF Birthday Parties: A Celebration Beyond Cake and Candles

In the mosaic of life's celebrations, few occasions hold as much sentimental weight and joyous anticipation as a birthday. "The Significance of Birthday Parties" aims to unravel the layers of meaning embedded in this seemingly simple tradition, exploring the profound impact it has on individuals, families, and communities.

Chapter 1: Origins and Evolution of Birthday Celebrations

- Historical Roots: Tracing the Origins of Birthday Parties

- The Evolution of Traditions: From Simple Gatherings to Extravagant Affairs

Chapter 2: Psychological and Emotional Impact

- Milestones and Reflection: How Birthdays Shape Identity

- The Role of Celebration in Mental Well-being

Chapter 3: Social Connection and Relationships

- Strengthening Bonds: How Birthdays Foster Social Ties

- The Rituals of Gift-Giving: Expressing Love and Gratitude

Chapter 4: Cultural Variances in Birthday Celebrations

- Global Perspectives: Diverse Traditions and Customs

- Unique Cultural Practices: Unraveling the Tapestry of Birthday Celebrations

Chapter 5: Personal Development and Growth

- Birthdays as Markers of Progress

- Celebrating Achievements: Acknowledging Success and Learning from Challenges

Chapter 6: The Role of Rituals and Traditions

- Cake-Cutting and Candle-Blowing: Symbolism in Birthday Rituals

- Creating Lasting Memories: The Importance of Traditions

Chapter 7: Planning the Perfect Birthday Party

- Venue Selection and Décor: Setting the Stage for Celebration

- Balancing Extravagance and Intimacy: A Guide to Thoughtful Party Planning

Chapter 8: The Future of Birthday Celebrations

- Navigating Changing Trends: Technology, Social Media, and Birthday Celebrations

- Sustainable Celebrations: Balancing Joy and Environmental Responsibility

As we embark on this exploration of the significance of birthday parties, we'll uncover the layers of meaning that make this tradition a cherished and enduring aspect of the human experience.

IF YOU HAVE SPECIFIC areas you'd like to explore further or specific details to emphasize, please let me know.

Chapter 1

Planning the Perfect Party

A. Setting the Stage

Choosing the Right Venue

Choosing the Right Venue: Crafting the Perfect Setting for Unforgettable Celebrations

In the symphony of event planning, the choice of venue orchestrates the melody that sets the tone for a memorable celebration. "Choosing the Right Venue" is not merely a logistical decision; it's an art form that requires careful consideration and expertise. Let's delve into the intricacies of selecting the perfect space to transform any occasion into an unforgettable experience.

Chapter 1: Understanding Your Event

- Defining the Celebration: Factors that Influence Venue Selection

- Tailoring the Venue to the Occasion: Birthdays, Weddings, Corporate Events, and More

Chapter 2: Assessing Capacity and Layout

- Capacity Considerations: Ensuring the Venue Accommodates Your Guest List

- Layout Dynamics: Maximizing Space for Comfort and Functionality

Chapter 3: Location Matters: Accessibility and Ambiance

- Proximity and Accessibility: Factors Influencing Venue Location

- Creating Atmosphere: Ambiance, Lighting, and Acoustics

Chapter 4: Budgeting and Cost Considerations

- Balancing Act: Allocating Budget for Venue and Amenities

- Hidden Costs: Navigating Pricing Structures and Negotiations

Chapter 5: Amenities and Services

- Venue Amenities: Beyond Four Walls

- Catering and Bar Services: Enhancing the Guest Experience

Chapter 6: Theme Integration and Customization
- Harmonizing Venue with Event Themes
- Customization Options: Turning the Venue into a Personalized Experience
Chapter 7: Legalities and Permits
- Navigating Contracts and Agreements
- Securing Permits: Ensuring Compliance and Smooth Execution
Chapter 8: Sustainability and Environmental Impact
- Eco-Friendly Venues: Navigating the Green Choices
- Minimizing Environmental Footprint: A Responsible Celebration
Chapter 9: Case Studies and Success Stories
- Real-Life Experiences: Learning from Memorable Celebrations
- Pitfalls to Avoid: Lessons from Challenges Faced
Chapter 10: Future Trends in Venue Selection
- Technology Integration: Virtual and Hybrid Venue Experiences
- The Evolving Landscape: What to Expect in Tomorrow's Venues

As we navigate the chapters, we will unravel the complexities of venue selection, empowering readers to make informed choices that elevate their celebrations to new heights.

Decorations that <u>Wow</u>

DECORATIONS THAT WOW: Elevating Celebrations with Aesthetic Brilliance

In the kaleidoscope of event planning, decorations emerge as the artistic brushstrokes that transform any venue into a canvas of celebration. "Decorations that Wow" is not merely a chapter in party planning; it's an exploration of the art and science behind crafting visually stunning environments. Let's embark on a journey to unravel the secrets of decorations that captivate, inspire, and leave an indelible mark on the memories of any gathering.

Chapter 1: The Psychology of Aesthetics
- Understanding the Impact of Visual Appeal on Celebration
- Color Psychology: Choosing Hues that Evoke Emotion
Chapter 2: Choosing Themes and Cohesive Design
- Crafting a Visual Narrative: The Role of Themes in Decoration
- Coordinating Elements: Achieving Cohesiveness in Design

Chapter 3: Balancing Scale and Proportion
- Space Dynamics: Adapting Decorations to Venue Size
- Proportionate Décor: Ensuring Harmony in Design Elements
Chapter 4: Lighting Magic: Techniques and Effects
- Ambient Lighting: Setting the Mood for Celebration
- Specialty Lighting: Adding Drama and Focus
Chapter 5: DIY Décor: From Concept to Execution
- Unleashing Creativity: The Art of Handmade Décor
- Budget-Friendly DIY Projects: Making a Big Impact with Limited Resources
Chapter 6: Floral Arrangements and Centerpieces
- The Language of Flowers: Symbolism in Floral Décor
- Elevating Tablescape: Crafting Stunning Centerpieces
Chapter 7: Sustainable Décor: Greening Your Celebration
- Eco-Friendly Choices: From Materials to Disposal
- Balancing Beauty and Environmental Responsibility
Chapter 8: Incorporating Technology in Décor
- Digital Displays: A Modern Approach to Décor
- Interactive Tech: Engaging Guests through Innovation
Chapter 9: Case Studies in Wow-Worthy Décor
- Memorable Décor Moments: Learning from Successful Events
- Pitfalls to Avoid: Navigating Challenges in Décor Planning
Chapter 10: Future Trends in Event Décor
- Virtual Décor: The Intersection of Technology and Aesthetics
- Sustainable Innovations: The Evolution of Eco-Friendly Décor

As we delve into "Decorations that Wow," we will uncover the principles, trends, and innovations that turn spaces into visually enchanting realms of celebration.

Navigating Guest Lists and RSVPs

NAVIGATING GUEST LISTS and RSVPs: The Art of Seamless Event Planning

In the intricate dance of event planning, mastering the guest list and RSVP process emerges as a skill that can elevate any celebration from ordinary to extraordinary. "Navigating Guest Lists and RSVPs" is not just about managing names on a page; it's about orchestrating a harmonious symphony of attendees, ensuring that every invitee feels welcomed and valued. Let's embark on a journey through the intricacies of curating guest lists and navigating the delicate art of RSVPs.

Chapter 1: Understanding the Purpose of Your Event
- Defining the Celebration: Aligning the Guest List with Event Objectives
- Differentiating Between Intimate Gatherings and Grand Affairs
Chapter 2: Crafting the Perfect Guest List
- Strategic Invitations: Balancing Personal and Professional Connections
- Guest List Size: Ensuring the Right Atmosphere for Your Event
Chapter 3: Invitation Etiquette and Design
- Communicating Tone: Crafting Invitations that Reflect Your Event
- Digital vs. Traditional: Choosing the Right Invitation Format
Chapter 4: The Art of RSVPs
- Importance of Timely Responses: Navigating RSVP Deadlines
- Creating User-Friendly RSVP Systems: Online and Offline Options
Chapter 5: Managing Responses and Dietary Preferences
- Tracking RSVPs: Tools and Strategies for Efficient Monitoring
- Catering to All Tastes: Handling Dietary Requests with Grace
Chapter 6: Dealing with Unexpected Changes
- Last-Minute Additions and Subtractions: Maintaining Flexibility
- Addressing No-Shows: Mitigating Impact on the Event
Chapter 7: Communication Strategies

- Clear Communication: Setting Expectations for Guests
- Gentle Reminders: Ensuring Response Promptness
Chapter 8: Leveraging Technology for Efficiency
- RSVP Apps and Software: Streamlining the Process
- Digital Solutions: Enhancing Communication and Coordination
Chapter 9: Case Studies in Guest List Mastery
- Success Stories: Learning from Well-Executed Guest List Management
- Lessons from Challenges: Navigating Common Pitfalls
Chapter 10: Future Trends in Guest List Management
- AI Integration: The Evolving Role of Technology in Event Planning
- Personalization and Customization: Tailoring Invitations for a Unique Experience

As we delve into "Navigating Guest Lists and RSVPs," we will uncover the intricacies, strategies, and future trends that transform guest management into an art form, ensuring that every event unfolds seamlessly and leaves a lasting impression on all attendees.

IF YOU HAVE SPECIFIC areas you'd like to explore further or particular details to emphasize, please let me know.

The Art of Timing: When to Start and End the <u>Celebration</u>

THE ART OF TIMING: When to Start and End the Celebration

In the realm of event planning, the concept of timing is not merely a logistical consideration but a nuanced art that can elevate a celebration from ordinary to extraordinary. "The Art of Timing" delves into the intricate dance of when to commence and conclude a celebration, exploring the subtleties that transform moments into lasting memories.

Chapter 1: Setting the Stage with Punctuality

- The Impact of Timeliness: Creating a Positive First Impression

- Coordination and Synchronization: The Role of Punctuality in Event Flow

Chapter 2: The Influence of Cultural and Regional Dynamics

- Understanding Cultural Perspectives on Timing

- Regional Variations: Navigating Different Approaches to Time

Chapter 3: Balancing Day and Night Events

- The Magic of Daytime Celebrations: Maximizing Natural Light

- Nighttime Revelry: Creating an Ambiance under the Stars

Chapter 4: Timing According to Event Type

- Corporate Events: Finding the Optimal Balance for Productivity and Enjoyment

- Social Gatherings: Tailoring Timing to Reflect the Occasion

Chapter 5: Strategic Scheduling for Maximum Engagement

- Key Moments: Timing Speeches, Performances, and Surprises

- Sequencing Events: Building Momentum throughout the Celebration

Chapter 6: The Psychology of Timing in Food and Beverage Service

- Cocktail Hours and Appetizers: Setting the Tone for the Event

- Dinner Timing: Balancing Hunger and Anticipation

Chapter 7: Navigating Time Zones and Global Events

- Virtual Celebrations: Overcoming Challenges of Diverse Time Zones

- Hosting Global Events: Timing Considerations for International Audiences

Chapter 8: The Art of a Graceful Conclusion

- Crafting Memorable Endings: Last Impressions Matter
- Managing Departures: Ensuring a Smooth Conclusion to the Celebration
Chapter 9: Seasonal Considerations
- Weather Dynamics: Adapting Timing to Seasonal Changes
- Themed Events: Aligning Timing with Seasonal Vibes
Chapter 10: Case Studies in Timing Mastery
- Success Stories: Lessons from Well-Timed Celebrations
- Timing Mishaps: Navigating Challenges and Learning from Mistakes
Chapter 11: Future Trends in Event Timing
- Hybrid and Virtual Events: Timing Considerations in the Digital Landscape
- Innovative Approaches: Rethinking Traditional Notions of Celebration Timing

As we explore "The Art of Timing," we will uncover the subtleties, strategies, and future trends that transform the temporal dimension of events into a masterful symphony, orchestrating moments that linger in the hearts of attendees long after the celebration concludes.

If you have specific areas you'd like to explore further or particular details to emphasize, please let me know.

Chapter 2

Themes and Creative Concepts

Unleashing Your Imagination

Unleashing Your Imagination: Navigating the Boundless Realm of Creativity

In the symphony of human experience, imagination stands as the conductor, orchestrating the limitless possibilities that dance within the corridors of our minds. "Unleashing Your Imagination" is not merely an exploration; it's an invitation to embark on a transformative journey through the boundless realm of creativity. Let's embark together on a voyage to unlock the full potential of the human imagination.

Chapter 1: Defining Imagination and Creativity

- Understanding the Interplay: How Imagination Fuels Creativity

- Breaking Misconceptions: Dispelling Myths About Creative Abilities

Chapter 2: Tapping into Personal Creativity

- Identifying Individual Strengths: The Unique Landscape of Imagination

- Overcoming Creative Blocks: Navigating Challenges on the Path to Innovation

Chapter 3: The Role of Imagination in Problem Solving

- Imagination as a Catalyst for Innovative Solutions

- Integrating Creative Thinking into Everyday Challenges

Chapter 4: The Connection Between Imagination and Well-being

- Mental Health and Imagination: A Reciprocal Relationship

- Imagination as a Therapeutic Outlet: Art, Expression, and Healing

Chapter 5: Cultivating a Creative Mindset

- Fostering a Growth Mindset: Embracing Challenges and Learning

- Creating an Environment Conducive to Imagination

Chapter 6: The Power of Play and Exploration

- Embracing Playfulness: A Gateway to Unrestricted Imagination

- Exploring New Horizons: How Curiosity Drives Creative Discovery

Chapter 7: Imagination in Various Forms of Art

- Visual Arts: Painting, Sculpture, and Beyond

- Literary Arts: Crafting Worlds with Words

- Performing Arts: Theatrical Expression and Dance

Chapter 8: Imagination in Technology and Innovation

- Technological Advancements: A Product of Human Imagination

- Innovations Shaped by Creative Visionaries

Chapter 9: Overcoming Fear of Failure

- Embracing Mistakes: The Path to Breakthroughs

- Learning from Setbacks: Resilience in the Face of Challenges

Chapter 10: Case Studies in Creative Brilliance

- Examining Iconic Creators: Their Processes and Inspirations

- Learning from Creative Masters: Translating Insights into Personal Practice

Chapter 11: Future Frontiers of Imagination

- AI and Imagination: Exploring the Intersection of Technology and Creativity

- Collective Imagination: Harnessing Group Creativity for Global Innovation

As we traverse the chapters of "Unleashing Your Imagination," we will not only explore the intricacies of creativity but also ignite the spark that transforms the ordinary into the extraordinary, inviting readers to embark on a journey of self-discovery and limitless possibility.

Thematic Elements that Resonate

THEMATIC ELEMENTS THAT Resonate: Crafting Memorable Celebrations

In the tapestry of event planning, themes emerge as the vibrant threads that weave a narrative, transforming gatherings into immersive experiences. "Thematic Elements that Resonate" is not just about selecting colors and decorations; it's a profound exploration into the art of choosing themes that captivate, inspire, and leave a lasting imprint on the memories of attendees. Let's delve into the intricacies of selecting thematic elements that transcend the ordinary and elevate celebrations to extraordinary heights.

Chapter 1: The Significance of Themes in Events

- Understanding the Impact of Thematic Elements on Attendee Experience

- Themes Beyond Decorations: How They Shape Atmosphere and Engagement

Chapter 2: Aligning Themes with Event Objectives

- Defining the Purpose: How Themes Enhance Event Messaging

- Corporate Events: Balancing Professionalism with Creative Expression

Chapter 3: Timeless Classics and Contemporary Trends

- Navigating Traditional Themes: Relevance in Modern Celebrations

- Trendspotting: Embracing Contemporary Themes for a Fresh Perspective

Chapter 4: Crafting Unique and Customized Themes

- Personalized Themes: Connecting Celebrations to Individual Stories

- Tailoring Themes to Diverse Audiences and Occasions

Chapter 5: Thematic Elements Across Cultures

- Global Inspiration: Exploring Themes from Different Cultural Perspectives

- Culturally Sensitive Themes: Balancing Authenticity and Respect

Chapter 6: The Role of Colors, Decor, and Invitations in Theme Execution

- Color Psychology: The Impact of Hues on Atmosphere and Mood

- Theme Integration: Coordinating Decor and Invitations for Cohesiveness

Chapter 7: Interactivity and Engagement within Themes

- Creating Immersive Experiences: Encouraging Attendee Participation

- Thematic Activities: Enhancing Engagement and Entertainment
Chapter 8: Transitioning Between Multiple Themes
- Dynamic Events: Successfully Incorporating Multiple Themes
- Fluid Transitions: Ensuring Cohesiveness in Theme Changes
Chapter 9: Thematic Challenges and Solutions
- Navigating Theme Limitations: Overcoming Venue and Budget Constraints
- Managing Guest Expectations: Striking the Right Balance in Theme Execution
Chapter 10: Case Studies in Theme Mastery
- Success Stories: Examining Unforgettable Events and Their Themes
- Learning from Challenges: Extracting Lessons from Thematic Mishaps
Chapter 11: Future Trends in Event Themes
- Technology Integration: Augmented Reality, Virtual Themes, and Beyond
- Sustainability and Themes: Balancing Creativity with Environmental Responsibility

As we explore "Thematic Elements that Resonate," we will unravel the intricacies, strategies, and future trends that make selecting and executing themes a transformative art, ensuring that every celebration becomes a memorable and immersive experience.

Timeless <u>Classics</u>

TIMELESS CLASSICS: A Celebration of Enduring Elegance and Style

In the ever-evolving landscape of trends and fads, there exists a realm where certain elements stand unyielding to the passage of time. "Timeless Classics" is not merely a glimpse into the past; it's a tribute to those enduring elements that continue to captivate hearts and minds across generations. Let's embark on a journey through the annals of style, elegance, and cultural resonance that define what it means to be timeless.

Chapter 1: The Essence of Timelessness
- Defining Timeless Classics: Elements that Withstand the Test of Time
- The Cultural Significance: How Timeless Classics Transcend Generations

Chapter 2: Fashion Icons and Timeless Elegance
- Wardrobe Staples: The Timeless Pieces that Define Elegance
- Style Icons: Embracing Fashion that Resonates Through Decades

Chapter 3: Enduring Beauty in Architecture
- Architectural Marvels: Buildings That Capture the Imagination Across Eras
- The Timeless Allure of Traditional Design: Balancing Heritage and Modernity

Chapter 4: Timeless Literature and Literary Themes
- Classic Novels: Stories That Continue to Resonate with Readers
- Universal Themes: The Threads That Bind Timeless Stories

Chapter 5: Iconic Films and Cinematic Legacy
- Cinematic Masterpieces: Movies That Transcend Trends
- The Enduring Appeal of Classic Film Genres

Chapter 6: Timeless Music and Melodies
- Musical Legends: Artists Whose Impact Echoes Through Time
- The Anatomy of a Timeless Song: Themes and Melodies That Endure

Chapter 7: Ageless Design and Decor
- Timeless Interiors: Elements That Bring Grace and Charm to Spaces

- The Evolution of Decor Styles: Blending Tradition with Contemporary Flair

Chapter 8: Timeless Traditions and Rituals

- Cultural Practices: Celebrations and Customs That Stand Unchanged

- Family Traditions: Passing Down Timeless Values Through Generations

Chapter 9: Navigating the Line Between Classic and Outdated

- The Pitfalls of Stagnation: Recognizing When to Adapt While Preserving Timelessness

- Balancing Tradition and Innovation: Ensuring Relevance without Compromising Classic Appeal

Chapter 10: Case Studies in Timeless Mastery

- Examining Brands and Icons That Have Stood the Test of Time

- Learning from Mistakes: Instances Where Timelessness Was Challenged

Chapter 11: Future Frontiers of Timelessness

- The Intersection of Technology and Tradition: Navigating the Digital Age

- Sustainability and Timeless Design: Crafting a Future of Enduring Elegance

As we explore "Timeless Classics," we will traverse the realms of culture, art, and design, unveiling the secrets of enduring beauty and style that continue to inspire and resonate, defying the boundaries of time.

Trendy and Unique Themes

TRENDY AND UNIQUE THEMES: Elevating Celebrations with Contemporary Flair

In the ever-evolving landscape of event planning, the pulse of innovation beats within the realm of trendy and unique themes. "Trendy and Unique Themes" is not just a guide; it's an exploration of the dynamic and creative currents that define modern celebrations. Join me on a journey through the exciting world of themes that break the mold, setting the stage for unforgettable and Instagram-worthy events.

Chapter 1: The Rise of Trendsetting Themes

- Defining Contemporary Trends: Elements that Captivate Today's Audience

- The Influence of Social Media: How Platforms Shape Event Aesthetics

Chapter 2: Embracing Pop Culture Phenomena

- From TV Shows to Memes: How Pop Culture Inspires Event Themes

- Navigating the Fine Line: Between Trendy and Short-Lived

Chapter 3: Modernizing Traditional Themes

- Time-Honored Customs in a Fresh Light: Blending Tradition with Contemporary Flair

- The Global Fusion: Merging Cultures for Unique and Trendy Celebrations

Chapter 4: Eco-Friendly and Sustainable Themes

- The Green Revolution: Sustainable Choices in Event Planning

- Incorporating Eco-Friendly Elements: From Decor to Favors

Chapter 5: Technology-Infused Experiences

- Virtual and Augmented Reality: Transforming Events into Digital Realms

- Interactive Tech: Engaging Guests with Innovative Experiences

Chapter 6: Whimsical and Fantasy Themes

- Fairytales and Beyond: Crafting Magical Worlds for All Ages

- Balancing Whimsy with Elegance: Creating Enchanting Event Spaces

Chapter 7: Art and Design Influences

- Art-Inspired Events: From Classic Masterpieces to Modern Movements

- Architectural Wonders: Translating Iconic Designs into Event Themes

Chapter 8: Destination-Inspired Celebrations

- Bringing the World to Your Event: Themes Inspired by Global Destinations

- Incorporating Cultural Nuances: Respectful and Authentic Destination Themes

Chapter 9: The Role of Fashion in Event Themes

- Runway to Event Space: Translating Fashion Trends into Themes

- Style Icons and Event Inspirations: From Retro Vibes to Avant-Garde

Chapter 10: Interactive and Participatory Themes

- Immersive Experiences: Themes That Encourage Active Participation

- Creating Lasting Memories: How Interactive Elements Enhance Events

Chapter 11: Case Studies in Trendsetting

- Analyzing Successful Events: What Worked and Why

- Learning from Less Successful Attempts: Identifying Pitfalls and Challenges

Chapter 12: Future Trends in Event Themes

- The Intersection of Sustainability and Technology: A Glimpse into Tomorrow's Celebrations

- Evolving Cultural Influences: Anticipating the Next Wave of Trendsetting Themes

As we journey through "Trendy and Unique Themes," we'll unravel the secrets of contemporary event aesthetics, exploring the balance between innovation and timeless appeal, and paving the way for celebrations that leave a lasting imprint on the collective memory.

If you have specific areas you'd like to explore further or particular details to emphasize, please let me know.

Chapter 3

Culinary Delights

A Feast for the Senses

Feast for the Senses: Crafting Culinary Experiences Beyond Taste
In the world of gastronomy, a meal transcends mere sustenance; it becomes an orchestration of flavors, aromas, textures, and visuals—a symphony that engages all the senses. "A Feast for the Senses" is not just a journey through culinary delights; it's an exploration of the art and science behind creating immersive dining experiences that leave a lasting imprint on the senses. Join me as we delve into the multifaceted world of gastronomy, where each dish tells a story, and every meal is a celebration of sensory indulgence.

Chapter 1: The Multisensory Culinary Experience

- Beyond Taste: Understanding the Role of Scent, Sight, Touch, and Sound

- The Psychology of Flavor Perception: How Our Senses Shape Culinary Enjoyment

Chapter 2: The Visual Artistry of Culinary Presentation

- Plating Techniques: Transforming Ingredients into Visual Masterpieces

- Color Psychology: How Hues Influence Perception and Appetite

Chapter 3: Scent and Aromas in Gastronomy

- The Olfactory Journey: How Aromas Elicit Emotions and Memories

- Pairing Scents with Flavors: Enhancing the Dining Experience

Chapter 4: Texture and Tactile Sensations

- Mouthfeel Mastery: Crafting Dishes with Diverse Textures

- The Pleasure of Touch: How Tactile Experiences Elevate Culinary Enjoyment

Chapter 5: The Symphony of Sound in Dining

- Background Music: Setting the Ambiance for Culinary Delight

- Culinary Performances: Live Cooking and Interactive Experiences

Chapter 6: Harmonizing Flavors and Umami

- The Basics of Flavor Pairing: Creating Balanced and Exciting Dishes
- Umami: The Fifth Taste and its Role in Culinary Satisfaction
Chapter 7: Seasonal and Locally Sourced Ingredients
- Celebrating the Earth's Bounty: Crafting Menus Aligned with Seasons
- The Impact of Locally Sourced Ingredients on Flavor and Sustainability
Chapter 8: The Influence of Cultural and Global Cuisines
- Cultural Fusion: Blending Traditional and Contemporary Culinary Elements
- Global Influences: How Different Cuisines Contribute to Culinary Diversity
Chapter 9: Immersive Dining Environments
- The Role of Ambiance: Creating Memorable Settings for Culinary Journeys
- Pop-Up Restaurants and Themed Experiences: Adding a Layer of Adventure to Dining
Chapter 10: The Art of Food Pairing
- Wine and Beyond: Matching Beverages to Enhance Culinary Experiences
- Experimental Pairings: Exploring Unconventional Matches for Bold Flavors
Chapter 11: Case Studies in Sensory Mastery
- Examining Restaurants and Chefs Known for Their Sensory Innovation
- Learning from Failures: Instances Where Sensory Experiences Fell Short
Chapter 12: The Future of Culinary Sensory Exploration
- Technological Advancements: How Innovation is Shaping the Future of Dining
- The Intersection of Wellness and Gastronomy: A Glimpse into Healthy Sensory Indulgence

As we embark on the pages of "A Feast for the Senses," we'll unravel the secrets of culinary artistry, exploring how chefs and gastronomic innovators create immersive experiences that resonate far beyond the palate. Each dish becomes a story, and every meal, a sensory celebration.

Tailoring Menus to Suit Every Palate

TAILORING MENUS TO Suit Every Palate: A Culinary Symphony of Inclusivity

In the realm of gastronomy, the art of crafting a menu extends beyond a mere collection of dishes; it transforms into a harmonious composition that caters to diverse tastes, preferences, and dietary needs. "Tailoring Menus to Suit Every Palate" is not just a guide; it's an exploration of the intricacies involved in creating culinary experiences that resonate with a broad spectrum of diners. Join me as we delve into the delicate dance of flavors, textures, and cultural influences that define a menu designed for inclusivity.

Chapter 1: Understanding the Diverse Palates of Your Audience

- Beyond Taste Preferences: Considering Dietary Restrictions and Allergies

- Cultural Influences: How Backgrounds Shape Culinary Expectations

Chapter 2: The Role of Dietary Trends and Lifestyle Choices

- Navigating the World of Diets: From Keto to Veganism

- Balancing Healthy Options with Indulgent Treats: Meeting Varied Lifestyle Preferences

Chapter 3: Crafting a Versatile Menu Foundation

- The Core Elements of a Diverse Menu: Staples That Appeal to All

- Adaptable Recipes: How to Modify Dishes Without Compromising Authenticity

Chapter 4: Innovative Fusion: Merging Culinary Traditions

- Exploring Fusion Cuisine: Creatively Combining Different Culinary Styles

- Fusion Success Stories: Restaurants That Master the Art of Blending Flavors

Chapter 5: Small Plates and Shared Dining Experiences

- The Rise of Shared Dining: Encouraging Exploration and Community

- Crafting Tapas-Style Menus: Offering a Taste of Everything for Everyone

Chapter 6: Customization and Personalization

- Interactive Menus: Allowing Diners to Tailor Their Culinary Journey

- Balancing Customization with Operational Efficiency: A Chef's Challenge

Chapter 7: Addressing Dietary Restrictions with Elegance

- Gluten-Free, Nut-Free, and Beyond: Crafting Delicious Dishes Without Compromising

- Creating Allergy-Friendly Menus: Strategies for a Safe and Enjoyable Dining Experience

Chapter 8: Seasonal and Local Ingredients in Menu Planning

- Embracing Seasonality: How Fresh Produce Elevates Culinary Offerings

- Supporting Local Producers: Fostering Sustainability and Community Engagement

Chapter 9: The Art of Pairing: Beverages that Complement Diverse Menus

- Wine, Craft Beer, and Beyond: Selecting Drinks that Enhance the Dining Experience

- Non-Alcoholic Alternatives: Catering to Every Palate in the Beverage Selection

Chapter 10: Case Studies in Menu Diversity

- Analyzing Restaurants Known for their Inclusive Menus

- Learning from Challenges: Instances Where Menu Diversity Was Challenged

Chapter 11: Future Trends in Menu Tailoring

- Technology and Personalized Dining: Exploring Interactive Menu Experiences

- Global Influences: Anticipating Culinary Trends that Transcend Borders

As we venture into the pages of "Tailoring Menus to Suit Every Palate," we'll unravel the strategies and insights behind creating menus that celebrate diversity, ensuring that every diner finds a symphony of flavors that resonates with their individual tastes and preferences.

If you have specific areas you'd like to explore further or particular details to emphasize, please let me know.

KET

Cake Matters: The Centerpiece of Celebration

CAKE MATTERS: THE ART, Science, and Joy of Celebratory Confections

In the tapestry of celebrations, one element stands as the quintessential centerpiece, embodying joy, tradition, and the essence of the occasion—the cake. "Cake Matters: The Centerpiece of Celebration" is not just a journey into the world of confectionery; it's an exploration of the significance, craftsmanship, and cultural richness that cakes bring to our most cherished moments. Join me as we delve into the layers of history, technique, and creativity that make cakes an indispensable part of our celebrations.

Chapter 1: The Symbolism of Cake in Celebrations

- Beyond Dessert: How Cakes Symbolize Joy, Milestones, and Shared Moments

- Cultural Significance: Diverse Traditions and Rituals Involving Cakes

Chapter 2: A Brief History of Celebratory Confections

- From Ancient Rituals to Modern-Day Festivities: The Evolution of Cakes

- Cakes Across Cultures: Tracing Unique Practices and Symbolism

Chapter 3: Cake Design as an Art Form

- Sculpting Dreams: The Creative Process Behind Cake Design

- The Intersection of Culinary Expertise and Visual Arts: Crafting Edible Masterpieces

Chapter 4: The Science of Baking Perfect Cakes

- From Batter to Oven: Understanding the Chemistry Behind Baking

- Troubleshooting Tips: Navigating Common Challenges in Cake Baking

Chapter 5: Classic vs. Trendy: Exploring Cake Styles

- Timeless Elegance: The Allure of Classic Cake Designs

- Trendsetting Techniques: Embracing Contemporary Trends in Cake Decorating

Chapter 6: Iconic Cakes in History

- Royal Confections: Cakes That Marked Historical Events

- The Influence of Celebrity Weddings: Setting Trends in Cake Design

Chapter 7: Crafting Personalized and Themed Cakes

- Tailoring Cakes to Reflect Individual Tastes and Preferences

- Themed Cakes: Elevating Celebrations with Creative and Personal Touches

Chapter 8: Flavors Beyond Vanilla and Chocolate

- Exotic Flavor Profiles: Expanding Palates with Unique Cake Flavors

- The Role of Local Ingredients: Infusing Regional Tastes into Cake Recipes

Chapter 9: The Business of Cake: From Home Bakeries to Patissier Empires

- The Rise of Home Bakers: Navigating the Entrepreneurial Landscape

- Celebrated Patissiers: Iconic Names That Transformed the World of Cake

Chapter 10: Cake and Social Media: A Perfect Blend

- Instagram-Worthy Creations: The Impact of Social Media on Cake Trends

- Virtual Cake Communities: Connecting Bakers and Enthusiasts Worldwide

Chapter 11: Cake Fails and Lessons Learned

- Hilarious Mishaps: Learning from Common Cake Baking Mistakes

- Transforming Failures into Masterpieces: Resilience in the World of Cake

Chapter 12: The Future of Cake: Innovations and Trends

- Cutting-Edge Techniques: The Role of Technology in Cake Design

- Sustainable Practices: Exploring Eco-Friendly Approaches in Cake Baking

As we embark on the pages of "Cake Matters," we'll uncover the sweet symphony that unfolds in every cake—the craftsmanship, cultural resonance, and boundless creativity that make cakes not just desserts but timeless expressions of joy and celebration.

If you have specific areas you'd like to explore further or particular details to emphasize, please let me know.

Chapter 4

Entertainment Extravaganza

Music and Mood

MUSIC AND MOOD: THE Harmonious Connection That Shapes Our Emotions

In the symphony of life, music emerges as a powerful conductor, orchestrating the ebb and flow of human emotions. "Music and Mood" delves into the intricate relationship between the melodies that surround us and the tapestry of feelings they evoke. As we navigate through the profound impact of music on our emotional landscapes, join me on a journey exploring the nuances, psychology, and universal resonance of this harmonious connection.

Chapter 1: The Language of Emotions in Musical Notes

- Decoding Musical Expression: How Melody, Tempo, and Rhythm Convey Emotions

- The Cross-Cultural Universality of Emotional Responses to Music

Chapter 2: The Science Behind Music and Mood

- Neurochemistry of Harmony: How Music Influences Brain Activity

- The Power of Dopamine: Understanding the Pleasure of Musical Experiences

Chapter 3: Music as a Therapeutic Tool

- Healing Harmonies: Exploring the Role of Music in Mental and Emotional Well-being

- Music Therapy Modalities: From Clinical Settings to Everyday Applications

Chapter 4: Tempo and Genre: Matching Beats to Emotions

- Upbeat Vibes: The Energizing Effect of Fast Tempos

- Melancholic Melodies: How Slow Tempos Elicit Emotional Resonance

Chapter 5: Cultural Influences on Emotional Responses to Music

- Regional Music and Emotional Expressiveness: A Cross-Cultural Examination

- The Impact of Tradition: How Cultural Backgrounds Shape Musical Preferences

Chapter 6: The Soundtrack of Life: Music and Memory

- Musical Memory Triggers: Nostalgia and Sentimental Attachments

- Creating Personal Soundtracks: How We Use Music to Narrate Our Lives

Chapter 7: Music and Creativity: A Symbiotic Relationship

- The Muse in Melody: How Music Enhances Creativity

- Famous Creators and Their Musical Rituals: A Glimpse into Artistic Inspirations

Chapter 8: The Influence of Lyrics on Emotional Impact

- Beyond the Melody: Analyzing the Emotional Weight of Lyrics

- Lyricism Across Genres: From Storytelling to Poetic Expressions

Chapter 9: Music in Different Settings: Events, Films, and Beyond

- Creating Atmosphere: The Role of Music in Events and Celebrations

- Film Scores: Crafting Emotional Narratives through Musical Composition

Chapter 10: The Evolution of Musical Tastes Across Ages

- Generation Soundtracks: How Musical Preferences Shift Over Time

- Bridging Generational Gaps: Shared Musical Experiences That Unite

Chapter 11: The Intersection of Music and Technology

- Streaming Services and Personalized Playlists: Shaping Individual Musical Landscapes

- Technological Innovations: How AI and Music Platforms Revolutionize the Listening Experience

Chapter 12: The Future of Music and Mood Exploration

- Emerging Trends: Innovations in Music Composition and Production

- The Role of Virtual Reality and Immersive Experiences in Shaping Emotional Responses to Music

As we embark on the journey through "Music and Mood," we'll unravel the intricate threads that connect us to the melodies that echo our joys, soothe our sorrows, and paint the canvas of our emotions with the vibrant hues of musical expression.

Games and Activities for All Ages

GAMES AND ACTIVITIES for All Ages: A Playful Journey Through Lifelong Enjoyment

In the tapestry of human experience, the thread of play weaves a pattern that spans across generations. "Games and Activities for All Ages" is not just a compendium of leisure; it's an exploration of the diverse avenues that cater to the universal need for enjoyment, engagement, and social interaction. Join me as we embark on a playful journey, delving into the intricacies of games, activities, and pastimes that transcend age boundaries.

Chapter 1: The Essence of Play: Why Games Matter at Every Age
- Understanding Play as a Fundamental Human Experience
- The Cognitive, Emotional, and Social Benefits of Play for All Ages

Chapter 2: Traditional Games That Stand the Test of Time
- Board Games: Nurturing Strategy and Social Bonds
- Classic Card Games: A Deck of Endless Entertainment

Chapter 3: Outdoor Adventures for Every Generation
- From Tag to Treasure Hunts: Rediscovering Classic Outdoor Games
- Nature-Inspired Activities: Promoting Physical Health and Connection with the Environment

Chapter 4: Mind Games and Puzzles Across Ages
- Crossword Puzzles to Sudoku: Mental Challenges for Lifelong Engagement
- Chess, Checkers, and Beyond: Strategic Games for Intellectual Stimulation

Chapter 5: Digital Play: Navigating the World of Video and Online Games
- The Evolution of Video Games: From Arcades to VR Experiences
- Family-Friendly Online Games: Bridging Generational Gaps in the Digital Realm

Chapter 6: Creative Pursuits: Arts and Crafts for All Ages
- Crafting as Therapy: The Therapeutic Benefits of Artistic Expression
- DIY Projects: Fostering Creativity and Hands-On Learning

Chapter 7: Sports and Physical Activities for a Lifetime of Health
- From Yoga to Pickleball: Physical Activities Suited for Varied Fitness Levels

- Team Sports and Community Engagement: The Social Fabric of Sporting Events

Chapter 8: Tabletop Role-Playing Games: A Unique Realm of Imagination

- Dungeons & Dragons and Beyond: Exploring the World of RPGs

- The Social Dynamics of Role-Playing: Building Friendships and Collaborative Skills

Chapter 9: Social Games: Strengthening Bonds through Play

- Trivia Nights and Game Nights: Creating Social Connections through Play

- The Role of Multiplayer Games in Fostering Relationships

Chapter 10: Adapted Games for Diverse Abilities

- Inclusive Play: Designing Games for Individuals with Special Needs

- Adaptive Sports: Expanding Opportunities for Inclusive Participation

Chapter 11: Games for Mental Agility and Memory Enhancement

- Memory Games: Sharpening Cognitive Skills Across Ages

- Brain-Training Apps: Exploring the Efficacy of Mental Fitness Platforms

Chapter 12: The Future of Play: Innovations and Trends

- Gamification in Education and Work: The Integration of Play in Serious Contexts

- Technological Advancements: The Intersection of Virtual Reality and Traditional Games

As we traverse the pages of "Games and Activities for All Ages," we'll uncover the rich tapestry of leisure pursuits that bind generations together, fostering joy, camaraderie, and the timeless spirit of play.

Hiring Entertainment Professionals

HIRING ENTERTAINMENT Professionals: A Comprehensive Guide to Curating Unforgettable Experiences

In the realm of event planning, the selection of entertainment professionals holds the key to transforming an ordinary gathering into an extraordinary experience. "Hiring Entertainment Professionals" is not just a guide; it's a meticulous exploration of the art and science behind curating memorable moments that leave a lasting impression. Join me on this journey as we delve into the intricacies of choosing the right entertainers, ensuring seamless collaborations, and crafting events that resonate with every audience.

CHAPTER 1: THE ART of Event Entertainment
- Defining the Role of Entertainment in Event Experiences
- From Corporate Galas to Private Parties: Tailoring Entertainment to Occasion
Chapter 2: Identifying Your Audience and Setting the Tone
- Audience Profiling: Understanding Demographics and Preferences
- Establishing Event Atmosphere: Aligning Entertainment with Desired Ambiance
Chapter 3: Types of Entertainment Professionals
- Live Bands and Musicians: The Melodic Heartbeat of Events
- Comedians and Emcees: Injecting Humor and Energy into Gatherings
- Magicians, Illusionists, and Beyond: The Allure of Magical Performances
Chapter 4: Hiring Professional Speakers and Presenters
- Keynote Speakers: Inspiring and Informing Audiences
- Workshop Facilitators: Engaging Participants with Interactive Learning
Chapter 5: Collaborating with DJs and Music Producers
- Crafting Playlists for Every Occasion: The DJ's Artistry

- Live Music vs. DJ Sets: Navigating Musical Choices Based on Event Dynamics

Chapter 6: Dance Troupes, Choreographers, and Interactive Performances

- Elevating Events with Dance and Movement

- Engaging Audiences: Interactive Performances That Leave a Mark

Chapter 7: Assessing Entertainment Contracts and Agreements

- Legal Considerations in Hiring Entertainment Professionals

- Contractual Clarity: Protecting Both Parties in the Agreement

Chapter 8: The Importance of Rehearsals and Technical Soundchecks

- Ensuring Seamless Performances: The Rehearsal Process

- Technical Soundchecks: Mitigating Challenges for a Flawless Event

Chapter 9: Managing Logistics and Coordination

- Coordinating Entertainment with Event Timelines

- Ensuring Smooth Transitions: The Role of Event Managers in Entertainment

Chapter 10: Budgeting for Entertainment Excellence

- Allocating Funds Strategically: Balancing Quality and Affordability

- Negotiation Strategies: Securing Top-Notch Entertainment within Budget

Chapter 11: Post-Event Evaluations and Feedback

- Collecting Feedback: Gauging Audience Satisfaction

- Continuous Improvement: Learning from Each Entertainment Experience

Chapter 12: Trends and Innovations in Event Entertainment

- Virtual Entertainment Experiences: Adapting to Changing Times

- Technological Integrations: The Future of Immersive Event Entertainment

As we navigate the realms of "Hiring Entertainment Professionals," we will unravel the secrets to orchestrating events that resonate with audiences, crafting experiences that linger in memories long after the curtains close.

Chapter 5

Capturing the Moments

Photography Essentials

PHOTOGRAPHY ESSENTIALS: A Comprehensive Guide to Mastering the Art of Capturing Moments

In the ever-evolving landscape of visual storytelling, the mastery of photography is both an art and a skill. "Photography Essentials" is your compass through this captivating journey, offering a meticulous exploration of the foundational principles, advanced techniques, and creative nuances that define the craft of photography. Join me as we unravel the secrets behind stunning compositions, technical expertise, and the ability to freeze moments in time with artistic finesse.

CHAPTER 1: UNDERSTANDING Your Camera Gear
- Demystifying Camera Types: From DSLRs to Mirrorless Systems
- Navigating Lenses: Choosing the Right Glass for Every Shot
- Accessories and Gadgets: Enhancing Your Photographic Toolkit
Chapter 2: Mastering Exposure: The Key to Perfect Shots
- Aperture, Shutter Speed, and ISO: The Exposure Triangle Unveiled
- Metering Modes: Decoding Light Measurement for Optimal Results
- Bracketing Techniques: Ensuring Proper Exposure in Challenging Conditions
Chapter 3: Composition Techniques for Visual Impact
- Rule of Thirds and Beyond: Crafting Dynamic Compositions

- Leading Lines, Framing, and Symmetry: Elevating Your Visual Storytelling

- Understanding Color Harmony: Creating Vibrant and Cohesive Images

Chapter 4: The Art of Focus and Depth of Field

- Autofocus Systems: Leveraging Precision in Focusing

- Achieving Bokeh: Mastering Depth of Field for Artistic Effect

- Hyperfocal Distance: Ensuring Sharpness from Foreground to Background

Chapter 5: Lighting Mastery for Captivating Images

- Natural Light Techniques: Harnessing the Power of Ambient Illumination

- Artificial Lighting: From Flash to Continuous Light Sources

- Golden Hour and Blue Hour Magic: Maximizing Natural Lighting Conditions

Chapter 6: Post-Processing Magic: Editing and Retouching

- Introduction to Editing Software: Adobe Lightroom and Photoshop

- Color Correction and Grading: Enhancing Visual Aesthetics

- Retouching Techniques: Striking the Balance Between Natural and Enhanced

Chapter 7: Posing and Directing Subjects

- Portrait Posing: Guidance for Natural and Flattering Expressions

- Candid Photography: Capturing Authentic Moments Unobtrusively

- Working with Models: Communication and Collaboration for Successful Shoots

Chapter 8: Mastering Different Photography Genres

- Landscape Photography: Techniques for Stunning Scenic Shots

- Portrait Photography: Connecting with Subjects Emotionally

- Macro Photography: Exploring the Miniature World in Detail

Chapter 9: Legal and Ethical Considerations for Photographers

- Understanding Copyright: Protecting Your Creative Work

- Model Releases and Permissions: Navigating Legalities in Photography

- Ethics in Photography: Respecting Subjects and Context

Chapter 10: Building Your Photography Brand and Portfolio

- Crafting a Unique Style: Differentiating Your Photographic Voice

- Online Presence: Building a Portfolio Website and Social Media Strategy

- Networking and Collaboration: Connecting with the Photography Community

Chapter 11: Staying Inspired and Evolving as a Photographer

- Overcoming Creative Blocks: Strategies for Rediscovering Inspiration

- Lifelong Learning: Embracing New Techniques and Technologies

- Balancing Passion and Professionalism: Sustaining a Fulfilling Photography Career

Chapter 12: Future Trends and Innovations in Photography

- AI in Photography: Exploring the Intersection of Technology and Creativity

- Environmental Consciousness in Photography: Navigating Sustainability

- The Evolving Role of Visual Storytelling: Adapting to Changing Audience Expectations

As we embark on this journey through "Photography Essentials," I invite you to absorb the knowledge, hone your skills, and ignite the spark of creativity that will illuminate your path as a photographer.

DIY Photo Booths and Backdrops

DIY PHOTO BOOTHS AND Backdrops: Unleashing Your Creativity in Capturing Moments

In the age of smartphones and social media, photography has become an integral part of our lives. DIY photo booths and backdrops offer an exciting and accessible way to elevate your photography game, whether you're hosting an event or simply want to add a touch of creativity to your everyday moments. Join me on a journey through the art of crafting personalized photo experiences, exploring innovative backdrops, and creating DIY photo booths that leave lasting impressions.

CHAPTER 1: THE RISE of DIY Photo Experiences

- The Evolution of Photo Booths: From Traditional to DIY

- Why DIY? Exploring the Benefits of Crafting Your Photo Setup

Chapter 2: Tools and Materials for Crafting DIY Photo Booths

- Essential Tools: A Comprehensive Guide to What You'll Need

- Choosing the Right Materials: Balancing Aesthetics and Durability

- Budget-Friendly Alternatives: Crafting Without Breaking the Bank

Chapter 3: Designing Creative Backdrops for Every Occasion

- Tailoring Backdrops to Events: Weddings, Birthdays, and Beyond

- Incorporating Themes and Personalization: Making Backdrops Meaningful

- DIY Backdrop Inspirations: From Minimalist Elegance to Whimsical Charm

Chapter 4: Building a Portable DIY Photo Booth

- The Anatomy of a Portable Photo Booth: Structure and Design

- Incorporating Lighting: Ensuring Well-Lit and Flattering Photos

- Portable Printer Options: Turning Instant Snaps into Tangible Memories

Chapter 5: Crafting Interactive Elements for Engaging Photos

- Props and Accessories: Adding Personality to Your Photo Booth

- DIY Interactive Elements: From Flip Books to Animated GIFs

- Balancing Fun and Elegance: Creating Photo Experiences for All Ages

Chapter 6: Photography Tips for DIY Enthusiasts

- Mastering Composition: From Rule of Thirds to Creative Framing

- Posing Techniques: Guiding Subjects for Natural and Expressive Shots

- Overcoming Lighting Challenges: Achieving Professional Results

Chapter 7: Setting Up and Managing DIY Photo Booths at Events

- Planning the Layout: Optimizing Space for Maximum Engagement

- DIY Photo Booth Etiquette: Ensuring Smooth Operations at Events

- Troubleshooting Common Issues: From Technical Glitches to Uncooperative Props

Chapter 8: DIY Photo Booths for Virtual and Remote Celebrations

- Adapting to Virtual Gatherings: Bringing DIY Photo Fun Online

- Remote DIY Experiences: Crafting Memorable Moments Across Distances

- Utilizing Social Media: Sharing and Celebrating Together, Apart

Chapter 9: Capturing Moments, Creating Memories

- The Emotional Impact of DIY Photo Experiences

- Testimonials and Success Stories: How DIY Photo Booths Leave a Lasting Impression

- The Power of Personalization: Making Every Photo Count

Chapter 10: Safety Considerations and Guidelines for DIY Setups

- Ensuring Guest Safety: Hygiene Practices and Equipment Sanitization

- Compliance with Venue Regulations: Navigating Legal and Safety Requirements
- Weathering Unexpected Challenges: Preparing for the Unforeseen
Chapter 11: Trends and Innovations in DIY Photo Experiences
- AI and Augmented Reality: Elevating DIY Photo Booth Interactivity
- Sustainability in DIY: Exploring Eco-Friendly Materials and Practices
- Collaborations and DIY Communities: Sharing Ideas and Inspiring Others
Chapter 12: Your DIY Photo Journey: From Beginner to Expert
- Growing Your Skills: Continuous Learning and Exploration
- Building a Portfolio: Documenting Your DIY Photo Booth Adventures
- Inspiring Others: Sharing Your DIY Photo Wisdom with the World

As we embark on this exploration of "DIY Photo Booths and Backdrops," I encourage you to unleash your creativity, personalize your photography experiences, and craft moments that tell unique stories.

If there are specific aspects you'd like to delve into further or particular details to emphasize, please let me know.

Creating Lasting Memories

CREATING LASTING MEMORIES: A Comprehensive Guide to Cherished Moments

In the tapestry of life, moments of joy, love, and celebration weave together to form the fabric of our memories. "Creating Lasting Memories" is not just a book; it's an exploration into the art and science of crafting moments that linger in our hearts forever. As we delve into the intricacies of memory-making, this guide will provide insights, practical tips, and heartfelt advice on how to curate experiences that stand the test of time.

CHAPTER 1: UNDERSTANDING the Power of Memories
- Defining Memories: How Our Brain Encodes and Retrieves Experiences
- The Emotional Impact: Why Some Memories Resonate Stronger Than Others
- The Role of Memories in Shaping Our Identities
Chapter 2: Embracing the Present for Future Nostalgia
- Mindfulness and Memory: How Being Present Enhances Recall
- Savoring Moments: The Art of Appreciating the Now
- Balancing Technology: Capturing Memories Without Losing the Moment
Chapter 3: The Science of Creating Lasting Impressions
- The Neurochemistry of Memories: Understanding Dopamine and Oxytocin
- How Senses Trigger Memories: Sight, Sound, Smell, Taste, and Touch
- Navigating Positive and Negative Memories: Strategies for Embracing Both
Chapter 4: Crafting Meaningful Celebrations
- Birthdays, Anniversaries, and Milestones: Designing Moments That Matter
- Personalization and Thoughtfulness: Adding Layers of Significance
- Balancing Tradition and Innovation: The Recipe for Timeless Celebrations
Chapter 5: Photography as a Time Capsule

- The Art of Capturing Moments: Beyond Selfies and Posed Photos

- Organizing and Curating Photo Collections: Preserving Digital and Physical Memories

- Photography Tips for Creating Evocative Images

Chapter 6: Rituals and Traditions: An Anchor in Time

- The Power of Rituals in Memory Formation

- Establishing Family Traditions: Building a Legacy of Shared Experiences

- Adapting and Evolving Traditions: Keeping Them Relevant Through Generations

Chapter 7: Travel as a Memory-Making Adventure

- Exploring New Horizons: How Travel Enhances Memory Formation

- The Art of Souvenirs: Collecting Mementos That Tell Stories

- Traveling Mindfully: Balancing Exploration and Reflection

Chapter 8: The Impact of Relationships on Memory

- Social Bonds and Memory Formation: How Shared Experiences Strengthen Connections

- Navigating Memory in Relationships: Dealing With Positive and Challenging Moments

- Creating Group Memories: The Dynamics of Collective Recollection

Chapter 9: Balancing Digital and Analog Approaches to Memory

- The Digital Era: How Technology Influences Memory Creation

- The Allure of Analog: Rediscovering the Charm of Tangible Memories

- Integrating Both Worlds: Maximizing the Benefits of Digital and Analog

Chapter 10: Memory Preservation and Legacy

- Documenting Family Histories: An Investment in Future Generations

- The Role of Oral Histories: Preserving Personal Narratives

- Leaving a Lasting Legacy: How Memories Shape Our Impact on the World

Chapter 11: Coping with Memory Loss and Grief

- Understanding Memory Loss: Differentiating Normal Aging from Cognitive Decline

- The Healing Power of Memory: Coping Strategies for Grief

- Celebrating Lives: Turning Loss Into a Tapestry of Remembrance

Chapter 12: The Art of Reflection and Gratitude

- The Value of Reflection: How Looking Back Enhances Present and Future Moments

- Practicing Gratitude: A Gateway to Appreciating Everyday Memories
- Cultivating a Memory-Infused Lifestyle: Living Each Day with Intention
As we embark on this journey of "Creating Lasting Memories," may you find inspiration, guidance, and the profound joy that comes from crafting moments that etch themselves into the beautiful mosaic of your life.

Chapter 6

Inclusive Celebrations

Celebrating Diverse Backgrounds and Cultures

CELEBRATING DIVERSE Backgrounds and Cultures: A Tapestry of Shared Joy

In the vibrant mosaic of humanity, each thread represents a unique background, culture, and story waiting to be told. "Celebrating Diverse Backgrounds and Cultures" is more than a guide; it's an invitation to explore the richness of our global tapestry through the lens of celebration. As we navigate this journey, we will unravel the intricacies of diverse traditions, uncover shared values, and discover the universal language of joy that binds us all.

CHAPTER 1: THE ESSENCE of Cultural Celebrations
    - Defining Cultural Celebrations: Rituals, Festivals, and Traditions
    - The Role of Celebrations in Preserving and Evolving Cultures
    - Universal Themes in Cultural Celebrations: Love, Unity, and Communal Spirit
    Chapter 2: A Global Calendar of Celebrations
    - Diwali: The Festival of Lights Illuminating Diversity
    - Chinese New Year: Welcoming Prosperity and Renewal
    - Ramadan: Fasting, Reflection, and Eid Al-Fitr Celebrations
    - Hanukkah: The Festival of Lights in Jewish Tradition
    - Carnival: A Joyous Extravaganza Across Latin Cultures
    - Kwanzaa: Honoring African Heritage and Unity

Chapter 3: The Power of Cultural Exchange

- Cultural Fusion in Modern Celebrations: Blending Traditions for Global Unity

- International Festivals: Showcasing Diversity Beyond Borders

- Cross-Cultural Influences in Music, Art, and Fashion

Chapter 4: Navigating Sensitivity and Respect in Celebrations

- Cultural Appropriation vs. Appreciation: Finding the Balance

- Understanding Sacred Traditions: Respecting Boundaries

- The Role of Education in Fostering Cultural Understanding

Chapter 5: Culinary Delights from Around the World

- Exploring Global Cuisine: A Journey Through Flavors

- The Rituals of Sharing Meals: A Cross-Cultural Bonding Experience

- Fusion Foods: When Culinary Traditions Collide

Chapter 6: Traditional Attire and Adornments

- The Symbolism of Clothing: Beyond Fashion in Cultural Celebrations

- Traditional Adornments: Jewelry, Tattoos, and Body Art

- The Language of Colors: Significance in Various Cultures

Chapter 7: Music and Dance: Universal Expressions of Joy

- The Rhythms of Celebration: Diverse Beats Around the World

- Folk Dances: A Window Into Cultural Narratives

- The Influence of Cultural Music in Popular Global Trends

Chapter 8: Art and Craftsmanship Across Cultures

- Traditional Art Forms: From Paintings to Sculptures

- Handicrafts as Cultural Artifacts: Preserving Heritage

- The Intersection of Technology and Traditional Craftsmanship

Chapter 9: Celebrating Diversity in Personal Milestones

- Cultural Wedding Traditions: From Ceremonies to Attire

- Coming-of-Age Celebrations: Rituals Marking Adulthood

- Death and Mourning Practices: Honoring Cultural Perspectives

Chapter 10: Community Festivals and Collaborations

- Multicultural Events: Showcasing Diversity Locally

- Collaborative Celebrations: Embracing Unity in a Globalized World

- The Role of Communities in Preserving Cultural Heritage

Chapter 11: Preserving Endangered Cultures Through Celebration

- The Threats to Cultural Heritage: Language, Practices, and Traditions

- Initiatives for Cultural Preservation: Documenting and Sharing
- The Role of Celebrations in Revitalizing Endangered Cultures
Chapter 12: Embracing a Global Identity Through Celebration
- The Power of Shared Joy: Building Bridges Across Cultures
- Cultivating Empathy and Understanding Through Celebrations
- Celebrating Diverse Backgrounds as a Path to Global Unity

As we embark on this cultural odyssey, may the pages of "Celebrating Diverse Backgrounds and Cultures" serve as a guide, encouraging readers to embrace the beauty of our differences and find common ground in the universal language of celebration.

All-Ages-Friendly Activities

UNLOCKING THE JOY: A Guide to All-Ages-Friendly Activities

In the vibrant tapestry of life, joy knows no age boundaries. "Unlocking the Joy: A Guide to All-Ages-Friendly Activities" is your compass to a world of inclusive, engaging, and delightful pursuits suitable for individuals of every generation. From the young to the young at heart, this guide is crafted to infuse every moment with shared laughter, learning, and the sheer pleasure of being together.

CHAPTER 1: THE ART of Inclusive Activities
- Defining All-Ages-Friendly Activities: A Holistic Approach
- The Importance of Inclusivity in Activity Planning
- Tailoring Activities to Different Age Groups: Challenges and Solutions
Chapter 2: Outdoor Adventures for Every Generation
- Nature Walks and Hikes: A Breath of Fresh Air for All Ages
- Picnics: Merging Culinary Delights with Outdoor Joy

- Gardening: Cultivating a Love for Nature Across Generations

Chapter 3: DIY Arts and Crafts Extravaganza

- Crafting as a Bonding Experience: From Simple Creations to Masterpieces

- Recycled Crafts: A Sustainable Approach to Artistic Exploration

- Seasonal Craft Ideas: Celebrating Nature's Rhythms

Chapter 4: Culinary Adventures in the Kitchen

- Family Cooking Nights: Shared Meals, Shared Memories

- Baking Bonanza: Sweet Treats for All Ages

- Cultural Cooking Classes: Exploring Global Flavors Together

Chapter 5: Music and Movement for Every Beat

- Dance Parties: Grooving Across Generations

- Family Karaoke Nights: Unleashing Musical Talents

- Instrument Exploration: From Mini Maestros to Seasoned Players

Chapter 6: Storytelling and Reading Circles

- Bedtime Stories for All Ages: Creating a Literary Ritual

- Collaborative Storytelling: A Fusion of Imagination

- Book Clubs for Families: Sharing Literary Adventures

Chapter 7: Mindful Moments and Relaxation

- Family Yoga Sessions: Balancing Body and Mind Together

- Meditation for All Ages: Cultivating Inner Peace

- Intergenerational Relaxation Retreats: Unplugging and Reconnecting

Chapter 8: Gaming Galore: Board Games and Beyond

- Classic Board Games: The Timeless Appeal of Strategy and Chance

- Digital Games for All Ages: Navigating the Virtual Realm Together

- DIY Game Nights: Creating Personalized Challenges

Chapter 9: Seasonal Celebrations and Traditions

- Crafting Holiday Traditions: From Decorations to Festive Feasts

- Seasonal Festivals: Embracing the Spirit of Each Occasion

- Intergenerational Customs: Passing Down Cultural Celebrations

Chapter 10: Educational Expeditions and Learning Adventures

- Science Exploration: Hands-On Learning for All

- Historic Adventures: Unveiling the Past Together

- Nature Education Outings: A Classroom Without Walls

Chapter 11: Connecting Generations Through Technology

- Virtual Gatherings: Bridging Distances Through Video Calls

- Educational Apps for All Ages: Learning Through Screens
- Creating Digital Memories: The Art of Online Scrapbooking
Chapter 12: The Importance of Intergenerational Bonding
- Fostering Connections Across Ages: The Heartbeat of Family
- The Impact of All-Ages-Friendly Activities on Well-Being
- Building a Legacy of Shared Experiences: The Gift That Keeps Giving

As you embark on this journey of unlocking joy through all-ages-friendly activities, may each page inspire you to create lasting memories, strengthen connections, and revel in the simple yet profound pleasure of shared moments across generations.

Chapter 7

Gifts and Gratitude

Thoughtful Gift Ideas

THE ART OF GIVING: A Comprehensive Guide to Thoughtful Gift Ideas

In the tapestry of human relationships, the threads of thoughtful gestures and heartfelt presents weave a story of love, appreciation, and connection. "The Art of Giving" is your definitive guide to navigating the vast realm of thoughtful gift ideas, ensuring that every occasion becomes an opportunity to express your sentiments in the most meaningful way possible.

CHAPTER 1: THE POWER of Thoughtful Gifts
- Understanding the Emotional Impact of Gift-Giving
- How Thoughtful Gifts Strengthen Relationships
- The Art of Selecting Gifts Based on Recipients' Personalities
Chapter 2: Unwrapping Occasions: Gift-Giving Etiquette
- The Etiquette of Gift-Giving: Dos and Don'ts
- Navigating Cultural Sensitivities in Presenting Gifts
- The Role of Occasion-Specific Gift Etiquette
Chapter 3: Thoughtful Gifts for Special Milestones
- Celebrating Birthdays: Beyond the Ordinary Presents
- Anniversary Gifts: Expressing Everlasting Love
- Graduation Tokens: Inspiring Future Endeavors
Chapter 4: Personalized Presents: Adding a Touch of You
- The Allure of Customized Gifts

- DIY Gifts: Crafted with Love and Creativity

- Engraving and Personalization: Transforming Objects into Memories

Chapter 5: Thoughtful Gifts for Various Relationships

- Gifts for Romantic Partners: Igniting Sparks and Fostering Intimacy

- Friendship Tokens: Strengthening Bonds Beyond Words

- Navigating Family Dynamics: Presents That Speak to the Heart

Chapter 6: The Language of Flowers and Plants

- Symbolic Meanings Behind Different Flowers

- Gifting Potted Plants: A Breath of Fresh Connection

- Combining Flowers and Gifts for Extra Impact

Chapter 7: Culinary Delights: Gourmet Gifts That Impress

- Artisanal Treats: A Feast for the Taste Buds

- Crafting Personalized Gift Baskets: A Symphony of Flavors

- The Gift of Culinary Experiences: Cooking Classes and Beyond

Chapter 8: Mindful and Wellness Gifts

- Spa and Relaxation Gifts: Creating Serene Moments

- Thoughtful Wellness Gifts: Nourishing Body and Soul

- The Rising Trend of Mindfulness Gift Sets

Chapter 9: Technology and Gadgets: Modern Marvels as Presents

- The World of Smart Gadgets: Gifts for Tech Enthusiasts

- Exploring Wearable Tech: Fashionable and Functional Gifts

- Thoughtful Tech Gifts for All Ages

Chapter 10: Books and Literature: The Gift of Knowledge

- Thoughtful Book Selection: Navigating Tastes and Interests

- Personalized Bookmarks and Accessories: Enhancing the Reading Experience

- Book Subscription Services: The Gift That Keeps on Giving

Chapter 11: Gifts That Give Back: The Art of Philanthropy

- Charitable Donations in the Recipient's Name

- Eco-Friendly and Sustainable Gifts: A Compassionate Choice

- Supporting Artisans and Small Businesses: Gifts with a Purpose

Chapter 12: Thoughtful Gifts for Difficult Times

- Navigating Grief and Loss: Sensitive Presents for Comfort

- Get-Well Gifts: Uplifting Spirits and Offering Support

- Thoughtful Gestures During Challenging Moments

Chapter 13: The Thoughtful Art of Presentation
- Creative Gift Wrapping Techniques: Turning Packages into Art
- The Impact of Presentation on the Gift-Receiving Experience
- Thoughtful Enclosures: Crafting the Perfect Message

As you delve into the pages of "The Art of Giving," may you uncover the joy in thoughtful gift-giving, transforming each present into a cherished chapter in the story of your relationships.

Navigating Thank-You Notes

MASTERING THE ART OF Gratitude: A Comprehensive Guide to Navigating Thank-You Notes

In the intricate dance of social interactions, expressing gratitude stands as a timeless and essential step. "Mastering the Art of Gratitude" is your definitive guide to navigating thank-you notes with grace and sincerity. Whether acknowledging a thoughtful gift, recognizing a favor, or expressing appreciation for a kind gesture, this comprehensive guide ensures that your words convey genuine gratitude.

CHAPTER 1: THE POWER of Thank-You Notes
   - Understanding the Impact of Gratitude on Relationships
   - How Thank-You Notes Strengthen Social Bonds
   - Gratitude as a Pillar of Emotional Intelligence
   Chapter 2: Crafting the Perfect Thank-You Note
   - The Anatomy of a Thank-You Note: Structure and Components
   - Tailoring Your Message to Reflect Sincerity
   - Balancing Formality and Warmth in Your Expression
   Chapter 3: Types of Thank-You Notes
   - Expressing Gratitude for Gifts: Specifics Matter
   - Acknowledging Acts of Kindness and Favors
   - Thank-You Notes for Professional Settings: Navigating Workplace Gratitude
   Chapter 4: Timeliness and Etiquette of Sending Thank-You Notes
   - The Art of Promptness: Sending Thanks in a Timely Manner
   - Etiquette Guidelines for Various Occasions
   - Navigating Cultural Differences in Thank-You Note Timing
   Chapter 5: Digital Thank-You Notes: Navigating the Virtual Landscape
   - The Rise of Digital Gratitude: Email and Social Media

- Maintaining Personal Touch in Digital Expressions
- When to Choose Digital Over Handwritten Notes
Chapter 6: Handwritten vs. Typed Thank-You Notes
- The Timeless Elegance of Handwritten Notes
- Pros and Cons of Typed Thank-You Notes
- How to Choose the Right Approach for Different Situations
Chapter 7: Addressing Challenges in Thank-You Note Writing
- Expressing Gratitude in Challenging Situations
- Thanking for Non-Tangible Gifts: Words, Support, and Presence
- Crafting Thank-You Notes for Group Settings
Chapter 8: Personalizing Your Thank-You Notes
- The Impact of Personal Touch: Mentioning Specific Details
- Incorporating Humor and Creativity in Your Expressions
- Using Language That Resonates with Different Audiences
Chapter 9: Thank-You Note Pitfalls: What to Avoid
- Common Mistakes in Thank-You Note Writing
- Avoiding Generic Phrases: The Pitfall of Clichés
- Ensuring Your Gratitude Shines Through Without Overdoing It
Chapter 10: Teaching Children the Art of Gratitude
- Instilling Gratitude in Children: A Lifelong Gift
- Guiding Children in Crafting Thoughtful Thank-You Notes
- Creative Activities to Foster Gratitude in Young Minds
Chapter 11: Thank-You Notes in Business and Professional Settings
- Navigating Corporate Gratitude: Clients, Colleagues, and Superiors
- The Role of Thank-You Notes in Networking and Career Advancement
- Etiquette in Professional Appreciation
Chapter 12: Gratitude Beyond Words: Gift-Giving in Return
- The Tradition of Reciprocal Gratitude
- Choosing Appropriate Return Gifts
- Balancing Gratitude without Creating an Exchange Obligation
Chapter 13: The Thank-You Note as a Keepsake
- Preserving Thank-You Notes as Cherished Memories
- Creative Ways to Display and Store Gratitude
- The Timelessness of Reflecting on Thank-You Notes

As you embark on your journey to master the art of gratitude, "Mastering the Art of Gratitude" will be your trusted companion, guiding you through the nuances of expressing appreciation in various aspects of your life.

Chapter 8

Navigating Challenges

Managing Unexpected Hiccups

MASTERING THE UNEXPECTED: A Comprehensive Guide to Managing Hiccups with Grace

Life is a journey filled with unexpected twists and turns. "Mastering the Unexpected" is your indispensable guide to navigating through unforeseen hiccups with finesse and resilience. Drawing upon the wisdom of experienced problem-solvers and experts, this book equips you with strategies to tackle challenges, overcome obstacles, and emerge stronger on the other side.

CHAPTER 1: UNDERSTANDING the Nature of Unexpected Hiccups
- Defining Unexpected Hiccups: From Minor Bumps to Major Challenges
- The Psychological Impact: Coping with Surprise and Uncertainty
- Embracing a Mindset of Adaptability and Resilience
Chapter 2: Common Types of Unexpected Challenges
- Health-Related Hiccups: Navigating Sudden Illness or Injury
- Financial Curveballs: Strategies for Managing Unforeseen Expenses
- Interpersonal Challenges: Dealing with Unexpected Conflicts and Relationship Issues
Chapter 3: Strategies for Immediate Response
- Assessing the Situation: Gathering Information Quickly
- Developing a Calm and Collected Initial Reaction
- The Importance of Taking a Pause Before Responding

Chapter 4: Building a Support System

- The Role of Friends and Family in Providing Emotional Support

- Seeking Professional Guidance: When and How to Reach Out

- Fostering a Supportive Network: The Power of Community

Chapter 5: Decision-Making During Unexpected Challenges

- Weighing Options: Evaluating Short-Term and Long-Term Consequences

- The Art of Prioritization: Identifying What Truly Matters

- Involving Others: Collaborative Decision-Making for Better Outcomes

Chapter 6: Cultivating Resilience as a Life Skill

- Developing Emotional Resilience: Tools and Techniques

- The Connection Between Resilience and Mental Well-Being

- Learning from Setbacks: Turning Challenges into Opportunities

Chapter 7: The Unexpected in Professional Environments

- Adapting to Workplace Changes: Job Loss, Restructuring, or Unexpected Transitions

- Navigating Office Conflicts: Strategies for Effective Resolution

- The Role of Adaptability in Career Success

Chapter 8: Finding Opportunities Amidst Challenges

- Shifting Perspectives: Viewing Unexpected Hiccups as Learning Experiences

- Creativity in Problem-Solving: Turning Constraints into Catalysts

- Recognizing Hidden Doors: How Challenges Can Lead to New Opportunities

Chapter 9: Strategies for Long-Term Recovery

- Setting Realistic Expectations: Recognizing the Process of Healing

- Incorporating Lessons Learned into Future Decision-Making

- Celebrating Milestones: Acknowledging Progress in the Journey

Chapter 10: Coping Mechanisms for Emotional Well-Being

- Mindfulness and Stress Reduction Techniques

- The Role of Physical Activity in Emotional Resilience

- Connecting with Others: The Healing Power of Human Connection

Chapter 11: Unexpected Hiccups in Relationships

- Navigating Relationship Challenges: Communication and Understanding

- Rebuilding Trust After Unexpected Setbacks

- Growing Together: The Strengthening Power of Shared Experiences

Chapter 12: Preparing for the Unexpected
- The Importance of Having a Contingency Plan
- Building Financial Safety Nets: An Investment in Future Security
- Developing a Mindset of Continuous Learning and Adaptation
Chapter 13: Real Stories of Triumph Over Unexpected Challenges
- Inspiring Accounts of Individuals Who Overcame Seemingly Insurmountable Hurdles
- Lessons Extracted from Real-Life Experiences
- The Human Capacity for Resilience: Stories that Motivate and Encourage

As you delve into the pages of "Mastering the Unexpected," you'll gain insights, strategies, and inspiration to confront life's unexpected hiccups with confidence and resilience.

Handling Differing Expectations

NAVIGATING DIFFERING Expectations: A Guide to Harmonious Relationships

In the tapestry of human interactions, differing expectations can often be the threads that weave moments of joy or contention. Understanding how to handle these diverging hopes and desires is key to fostering healthy relationships and building bridges between individuals. In this comprehensive guide, we explore the intricacies of managing expectations, providing insights and strategies to navigate the delicate balance between various perspectives.

CHAPTER 1: THE DYNAMICS of Expectations

- Defining Expectations: Unveiling the Core Components
- The Role of Expectations in Relationships: A Double-Edged Sword
- How Expectations Develop: Unconscious Influences and Societal Norms

Chapter 2: Identifying Different Expectation Styles

- Intrinsic vs. Extrinsic Expectations: Internal Motivations and External Pressures
- Personal vs. Interpersonal Expectations: Balancing Self-Desires with Relationship Dynamics
- Short-Term vs. Long-Term Expectations: Navigating Immediate Needs and Future Plans

Chapter 3: Communication Strategies for Expressing Expectations

- Articulating Expectations Effectively: The Power of Clarity
- Active Listening: A Crucial Skill in Understanding Others' Expectations
- Non-Verbal Communication: The Subtle Language of Expectations

Chapter 4: Resolving Conflicts Arising from Differing Expectations

- Common Sources of Conflict: Money, Time, and Future Plans
- The Impact of Unmet Expectations on Emotional Well-Being
- Strategies for Constructive Conflict Resolution

Chapter 5: Finding Common Ground

- The Art of Compromise: Balancing Needs and Wants

- Establishing Shared Goals: Creating a Unified Vision

- Navigating Cultural and Value-Based Differences in Expectations

Chapter 6: The Psychology of Expectations

- Cognitive Biases in Perceiving Expectations

- The Influence of Past Experiences on Current Expectations

- The Role of Emotions in Shaping Expectations

Chapter 7: Building Trust Amidst Differing Expectations

- The Relationship Between Trust and Meeting Expectations

- Honesty and Transparency: Pillars of Trust in Relationships

- Strategies to Rebuild Trust After Unmet Expectations

Chapter 8: Managing Expectations in Professional Settings

- Navigating Workplace Expectations: Colleagues, Supervisors, and Career Goals

- The Intersection of Personal and Professional Expectations

- Balancing Ambition and Realism in Career Aspirations

Chapter 9: Expectations in Friendships and Social Circles

- The Dynamics of Social Expectations: From Casual Friendships to Close Bonds

- Handling Discrepancies in Social Expectations

- Building Stronger Connections Through Aligned Expectations

Chapter 10: The Impact of Technology on Expectations

- Social Media and Its Role in Shaping Expectations

- The Influence of Online Interactions on Personal and Professional Expectations

- Navigating the Digital Landscape: Healthy Boundaries and Communication

Chapter 11: Embracing Change and Adaptability

- The Inevitability of Change: How Expectations Shift Over Time

- Developing Flexibility in the Face of Evolving Expectations

- Cultivating a Mindset of Continuous Growth and Adaptation

Chapter 12: Real-Life Stories of Expectation Management

- Inspiring Narratives of Individuals Who Successfully Navigated Differing Expectations

- Lessons Learned from Real-Life Experiences

- The Human Capacity for Resilience: Stories that Illuminate the Path Forward

As you embark on this journey through the complexities of expectations, may this guide empower you with the knowledge and insights to foster understanding, harmony, and connection in all areas of your life.

Chapter 9

Sustainable Celebrations

Environmentally Friendly Practices

CHAMPIONING SUSTAINABILITY: A Comprehensive Guide to Environmentally Friendly Practices

In an era marked by environmental concerns and a growing awareness of our impact on the planet, adopting environmentally friendly practices has become an imperative. This book serves as a comprehensive guide, delving into the intricacies of sustainable living, green technologies, and eco-conscious choices. Let's embark on a journey to understand the importance of preserving our environment and the practical steps we can take to create a more sustainable future.

CHAPTER 1: UNDERSTANDING Environmental Sustainability
- Defining Environmental Sustainability: A Holistic Perspective
- The Interconnected Web of Nature: Why Sustainability Matters
- The Impact of Human Activities on the Environment
Chapter 2: The Role of Individuals in Environmental Conservation
- The Power of Personal Choices: How Individuals Contribute to Environmental Sustainability
- Everyday Eco-Friendly Habits: From Recycling to Reducing Energy Consumption
- Navigating Sustainable Consumerism: Making Informed Choices
Chapter 3: Sustainable Living Practices

- Eco-Friendly Homes: From Green Building Materials to Energy-Efficient Designs

- Water Conservation Strategies for Sustainable Living

- Gardening and Sustainable Agriculture: Cultivating a Greener Lifestyle

Chapter 4: Renewable Energy Sources

- Harnessing the Power of the Sun: Solar Energy Explained

- Wind Energy: A Clean and Renewable Resource

- The Potential of Hydropower and Other Emerging Renewable Technologies

Chapter 5: Sustainable Transportation

- The Environmental Impact of Traditional Transportation

- Exploring Eco-Friendly Modes of Transportation: Electric Vehicles, Bicycles, and Public Transit

- The Future of Sustainable Mobility: Innovations and Emerging Trends

Chapter 6: Green Technologies in Daily Life

- Smart Homes and Sustainable Technologies

- Sustainable Fashion: From Eco-Friendly Fabrics to Ethical Practices

- Innovations in Eco-Friendly Packaging and Waste Reduction

Chapter 7: Corporate Responsibility and Sustainable Business Practices

- The Business Case for Sustainability

- Companies Leading the Way: Examples of Sustainable Practices

- Sustainable Supply Chains and Ethical Business Conduct

Chapter 8: Conservation and Biodiversity

- Preserving Ecosystems: The Importance of Biodiversity

- Wildlife Conservation Efforts: Protecting Endangered Species

- Strategies for Balancing Human Development with Environmental Preservation

Chapter 9: Governmental Policies and International Cooperation

- Environmental Regulations: Shaping Policies for a Sustainable Future

- International Agreements and Collaborative Efforts

- The Role of Advocacy in Influencing Environmental Policies

Chapter 10: Overcoming Challenges in Sustainable Living

- Addressing Barriers to Sustainable Practices

- Inspiring Community Engagement and Collaboration

- Overcoming Psychological Resistance to Change

Chapter 11: Educational Initiatives and Raising Environmental Awareness
- The Importance of Environmental Education
- Inspiring the Next Generation: Environmental Awareness in Schools
- Leveraging Media and Technology for Environmental Education
Chapter 12: Real-Life Success Stories and Case Studies
- Profiles of Individuals and Communities Making a Positive Environmental Impact
- Lessons Learned from Successful Environmental Initiatives
- How Every Action, Big or Small, Contributes to Global Change

As we navigate through these chapters, may the knowledge within empower us to make informed decisions, adopt sustainable practices, and collectively contribute to the well-being of our planet.

Reducing Waste without Compromising Fun

MAXIMIZING JOY, MINIMIZING Waste: A Guide to Reducing Waste without Compromising Fun

In a world where sustainability is at the forefront of our collective consciousness, finding ways to reduce waste without sacrificing enjoyment is both a noble pursuit and an achievable goal. This book is your comprehensive guide to embracing a lifestyle that prioritizes fun and fulfillment while minimizing your environmental footprint. Let's embark on a journey together, exploring practical strategies, creative ideas, and inspiring examples to reduce waste in various aspects of our lives.

CHAPTER 1: THE IMPACT of Waste on Our Environment
- Understanding the Environmental Consequences of Excessive Waste
- The Importance of Individual Actions in Waste Reduction
- Connecting the Dots: How Waste Affects Biodiversity and Climate Change
Chapter 2: Mindful Consumption
- Conscious Consumerism: Making Informed and Sustainable Choices
- The Pitfalls of Fast Fashion and Single-Use Items
- Embracing Minimalism: Quality over Quantity
Chapter 3: Sustainable Practices in Everyday Life
- Waste Reduction at Home: From Kitchen to Bathroom
- Eco-Friendly Cleaning and Personal Care Products
- Navigating Sustainable Practices in Household Management
Chapter 4: Reducing Waste in Entertainment and Events
- Hosting Zero-Waste Parties and Events
- Sustainable Gift-Giving: Creative and Eco-Friendly Ideas
- Transforming Celebrations into Environmental Advocacy
Chapter 5: Traveling Light: A Zero-Waste Adventure

- Sustainable Travel Tips: Explore the World Responsibly
- Eco-Friendly Packing and Transportation
- Supporting Sustainable Tourism Initiatives
Chapter 6: Mindful Eating for a Greener Plate
- Embracing Plant-Based Diets for Environmental Impact
- Minimizing Food Waste: Meal Planning and Storage Tips
- Sustainable Dining Choices: Local, Seasonal, and Ethical Eating
Chapter 7: Waste-Free Hobbies and Leisure Activities
- Eco-Friendly Crafting: Turning Trash into Treasures
- Sustainable Gardening Practices
- Choosing Recyclable and Low-Impact Hobbies
Chapter 8: Greening Your Digital Lifestyle
- The Environmental Impact of Electronic Waste
- Sustainable Practices in the Digital Age
- E-Waste Recycling and Responsible Electronics Use
Chapter 9: Instilling Eco-Friendly Habits in Children
- Teaching Kids the Value of Waste Reduction
- Engaging Children in Sustainable Practices
- Eco-Friendly Toys and Games for Environmental Education
Chapter 10: Engaging Communities in Waste Reduction
- The Power of Collective Action: Community Initiatives
- Zero-Waste Challenges and Competitions
- Building Sustainable Partnerships: Local Businesses and Organizations
Chapter 11: Measuring Progress: Tracking Your Waste Reduction Journey
- Setting Achievable Goals for Waste Reduction
- Utilizing Apps and Tools to Monitor and Evaluate Progress
- Celebrating Milestones and Encouraging Continued Improvement
Chapter 12: Real-Life Success Stories and Case Studies
- Profiles of Individuals and Communities Making Strides in Waste Reduction
- The Economic Benefits of Adopting Sustainable Practices
- Lessons Learned from Successful Waste Reduction Initiatives

EMBARK ON THIS WASTE-reducing journey with the intention to create lasting change—where joy and sustainability harmoniously coexist. Let the exploration begin!

Conclusion

Conclusion: Paving the Way for a Sustainable Tomorrow

As we conclude this journey through the realms of waste reduction and sustainable living, it's paramount to reflect on the wealth of knowledge we've acquired and the transformative potential embedded in each conscious decision we make. The pursuit of reducing waste without compromising the joy in our lives is not just an individual endeavor; it's a collective movement shaping the future of our planet.

Throughout this book, we've explored multifaceted strategies for waste reduction, delving into the intricate balance between environmental consciousness and the pursuit of happiness. From the profound impact of mindful consumption to the intricacies of hosting zero-waste events, we've witnessed how small, intentional choices can create ripples of positive change.

Reflecting on Our Impact:

Understanding the environmental consequences of waste has been a crucial foundation for our journey. By realizing the interconnectedness of our actions with the broader ecosystems, we've laid the groundwork for meaningful change. Each piece of plastic reduced, every eco-friendly choice made, contributes to the preservation of our planet for future generations.

Mindful Consumption as a Way of Life:

The concept of conscious consumerism has emerged as a guiding principle. We've explored the pitfalls of fast fashion, the allure of minimalism, and the power of informed, sustainable choices. Embracing a lifestyle where quality surpasses quantity has proven not only environmentally responsible but also conducive to a more fulfilling life.

Sustainable Practices in Every Sphere:

From eco-friendly cleaning habits to travel practices that embrace responsibility, we've uncovered ways to integrate sustainability seamlessly into various aspects of our lives. The chapters on reducing waste in entertainment, sustainable eating habits, and waste-free hobbies have provided practical insights into achieving a greener, more conscious lifestyle.

Empowering Future Generations:

Our exploration extends beyond individual actions. Engaging children in eco-friendly habits and supporting community initiatives are vital steps toward creating a lasting impact. By instilling these values in the younger generation and fostering a sense of collective responsibility, we contribute to the longevity of our shared home.

Tracking Progress and Celebrating Success:

In our quest for sustainability, setting achievable goals and measuring progress is pivotal. Utilizing tools to monitor waste reduction efforts and celebrating milestones fosters a sense of accomplishment, reinforcing our commitment to the cause.

Inspiration from Real-Life Success Stories:

The real-life success stories and case studies showcased in this book serve as beacons of hope. Individuals and communities making strides in waste reduction demonstrate the tangible benefits and the ripple effect of sustainability initiatives.

A Call to Collective Action:

As we conclude, the message is clear: we are not isolated in this endeavor. Our collective actions, no matter how small, form a formidable force for positive change. This journey is a call to arms—a reminder that the choices we make today sculpt the world we inhabit tomorrow.

In conclusion, adopting environmentally friendly practices and reducing waste need not be a sacrifice; instead, it's an investment in a brighter, more sustainable future. The pursuit of joy and the preservation of our planet can go hand in hand. Let this be a call to action, an encouragement to spread awareness, and a commitment to ongoing improvement. Together, we pave the way for a tomorrow that is not only sustainable but thriving.

Note: This concluding chapter provides a summary and reflection on the key aspects discussed throughout the book,

fostering a sense of closure while encouraging continued commitment to sustainable practices.

www.ingramcontent.com/pod-product-compliance
Lightning Source LLC
Chambersburg PA
CBHW070032260726
48658CB00002B/593